For Nas

LAURENCE KING

First published in 2010 by
Eightbear Press, reprinted in 2012

This edition published in 2019 by
Laurence King Publishing Ltd
361–373 City Road
London EC1V 1LR
United Kingdom
Tel: +44 20 7841 6900
E-mail: enquiries@laurenceking.com
www.laurenceking.com

This book was produced by
Laurence King Publishing Ltd, London

A catalogue record for this book is available
from the British Library.

ISBN: 978-1-78627-561-5

Printed in Italy

Laurence King Publishing is committed to ethical
and sustainable production. We are proud participants in
The Book Chain Project ®
bookchainproject.com

Almost an
ANIMAL
ALPHABET

Katie Viggers

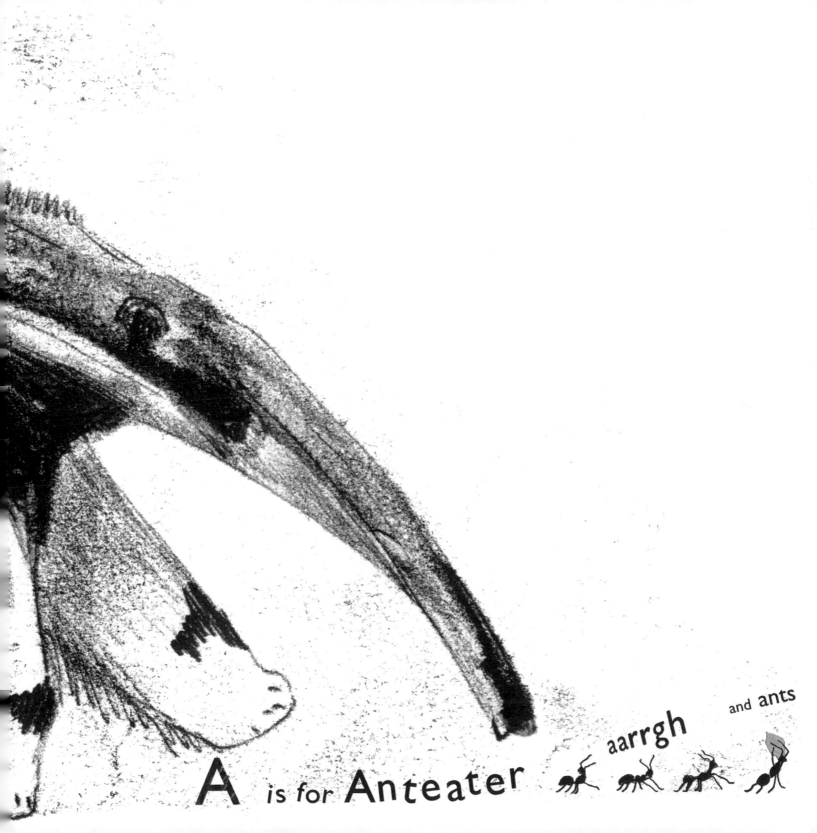

A is for Anteater   aarrgh   and ants

B  is for bears

polar

black
(Asian)

sun

spectacled

bamboo

brown

black
(North American)

sloth

panda

C is for

Cat

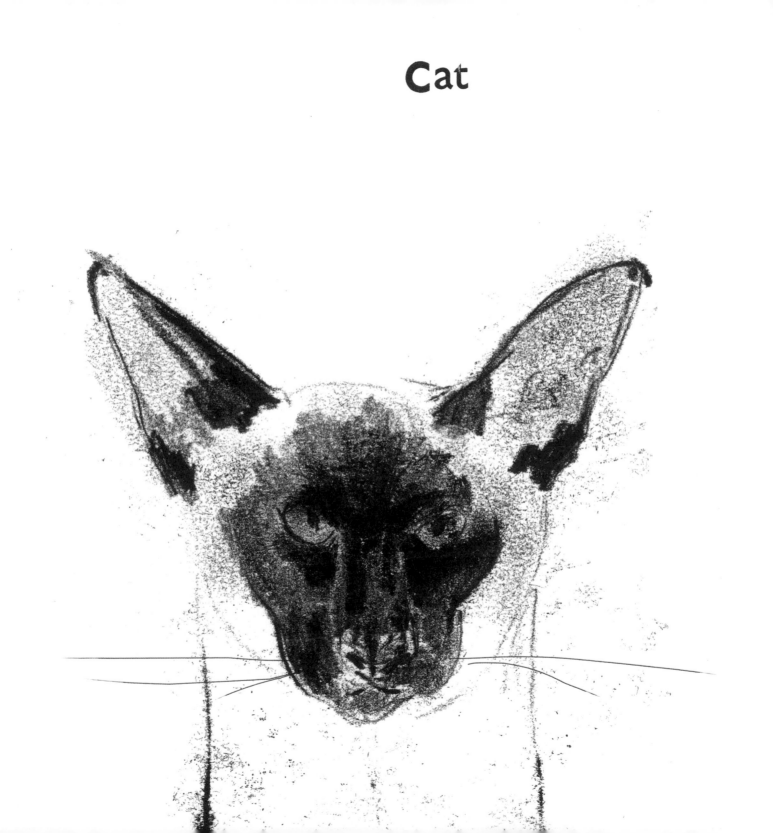

Triceratops

Tyrannosaurus rex

Stegosaurus

Pterodactyl

E is for **Elephant** *(Indian)*

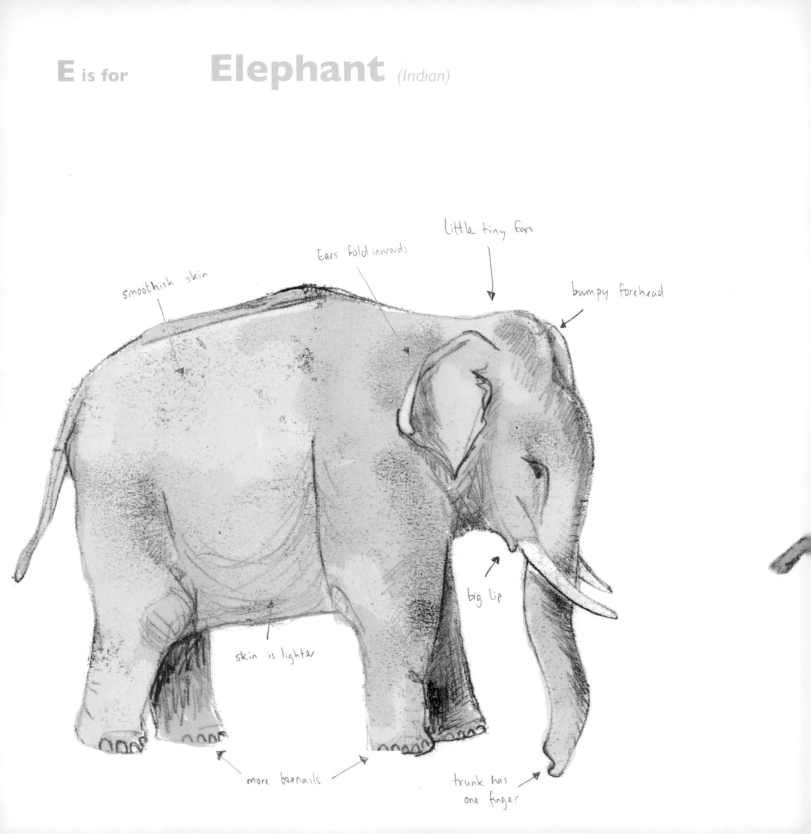

little tiny Ears

Ears fold inwards

smoothish skin

bumpy forehead

big lip

skin is lighter

more toenails

trunk has one finger

Elephant *(African)*

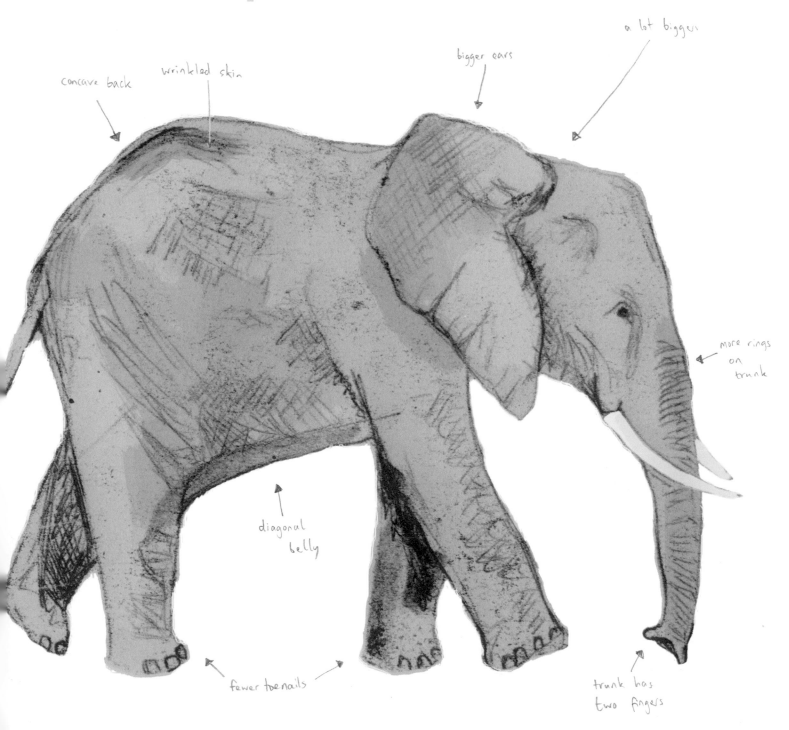

concave back

wrinkled skin

bigger ears

a lot bigger

more rings on trunk

diagonal belly

fewer toenails

trunk has two fingers

G is for Gorilla

H is for
Hammerhead
Shark

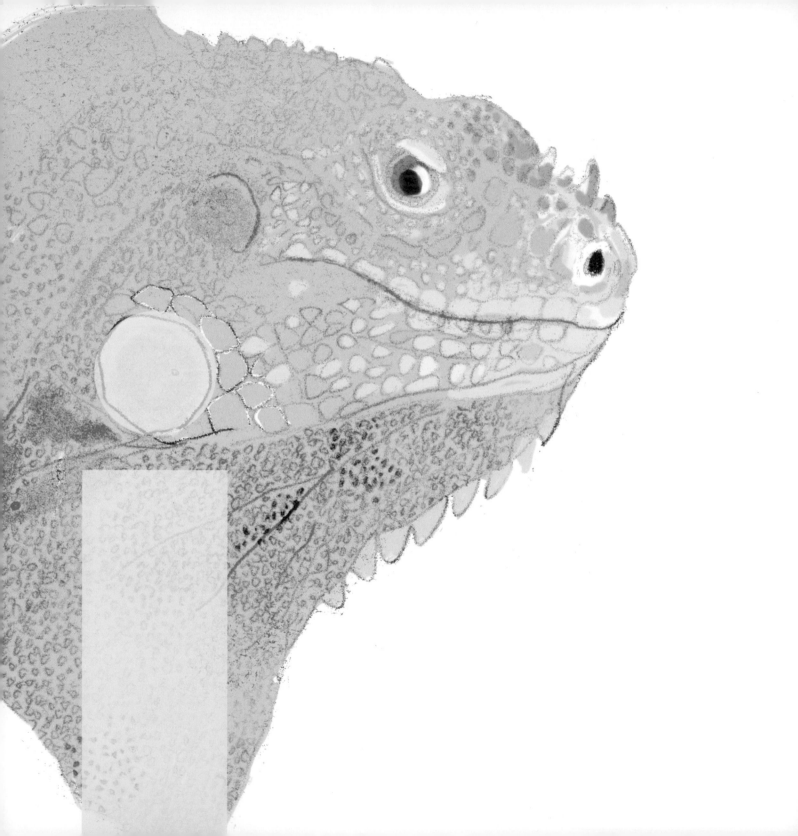

is for **iguana**

is for

K is for Koala

L is for Llama

capuchin

owl

colobus

spider

golden

mandrill

saki

is for Monkey

n is for night-time

Owl

screech

great grey

snowy

P is for Penguins

Galapagos

Little

long live
the king

Adélie

King

Fjordland

Rockhopper

Emperor

male

Q is for Quail

female

r is for reindeer

s is for sloth

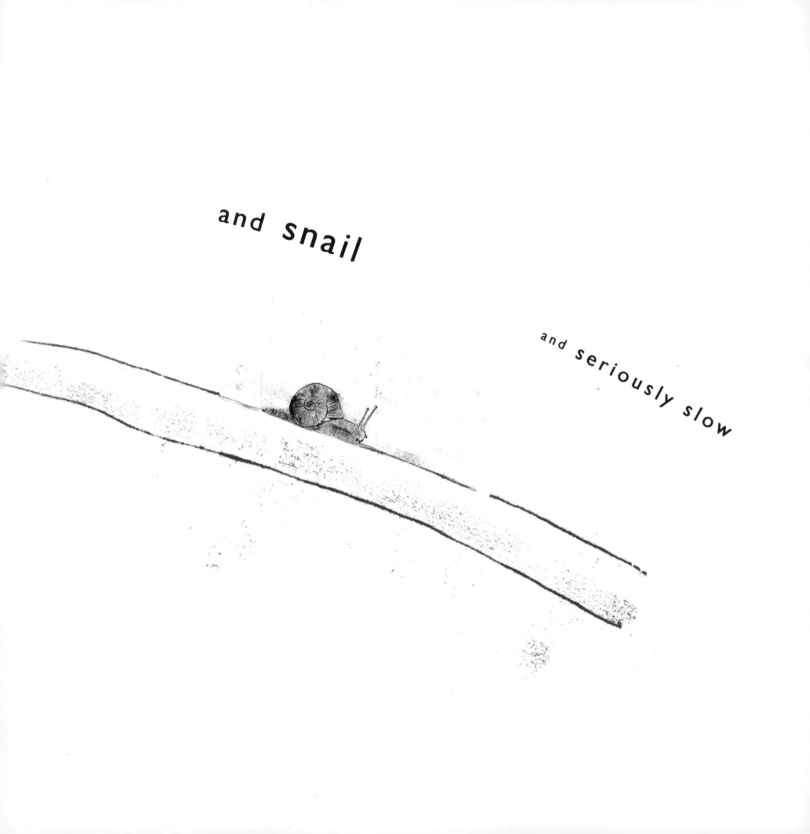

and snail

and seriously slow

t is for tarsier

is for **Underground**

v is for

Pondicherry

hooded

vulture

king

Rüppell's

W

is for

whale

x is for x-ray

Y is for Yeti

z is for zebra

KV is for Katie Viggers

Katie wrote this book

She is an artist who lives in london England

with her husband Nas and their 2 children.

.......and the red foxes!